Gerlind
Mégroz

HAND GLASS ENGRAVING

HAND GLASS ENGRAVING

a new hobby and homecraft

**Gerlind
Mégroz**

The photographs in this book are of hand engraved
glass, glassware and acrylic; designed and produced in
Switzerland by Gerlind Mégroz and her pupils
E. Gisiger, U. Hotz, M. Klotz, A. Landert, E. Ratzer,
E. Rhonheimer, S. Rinaldi, A. Schenkel, H. Schnabel and
T. Venanzoni.

This is a translation by Steve Jacobs from the original
text written by **Gerlind Mégroz**, one of the first
exponents of this hand glass engraving technique.

ISBN 0 9508084 1 5

Printed by Ted Ditchburn (Printing) Limited, Hatfield,
Herts., England

Contents

Introduction

The age-old art of glass engraving, almost forgotten for centuries, is being revived.

The rediscovery of this once exclusive craft is due to newly-developed diamond needles which are easy to use and make it possible for anyone, with or without artistic talents, to achieve remarkable success in a very short time.

Glass comes in many shapes, sizes and colours and the necessary tools and aids can be purchased from many good craft or hobby-shops. But remember that a good quality pattern is vital; not all patterns you can buy are really suitable.

This book tells you a great deal about hand engraving and will enable you to work successfully with glass to produce really impressive engravings, as we examine every detail, effect and possibility with the aid of full-colour illustrations.

Experience has shown that glass engraving is the kind of hobby which proves a delight to those who try it, not least because it is so simple to produce something really special. Which is why you will, without doubt, find it just as fascinating.

For many people it is important that their hobby does not involve great expense and can, like glass engraving, be enjoyed anywhere, anytime—even when they have only a few moments to spare.

Glass engraving opens up a whole variety of possibilities and opportunities, enabling you to give pleasure to relatives and friends alike with gifts of your own making.

Glass Engraving yesterday and today

"Souvent femme varie!" These words on the unpredictability of women are said to have been etched by King Franz I with his diamond ring into one of the windows of the Chambord, his chateau on the Loire. In 1456 Ludwig van Berquem discovered that one diamond could be polished using the dust of another. About a hundred years later, someone—probably in Venice—hit upon the idea of using a diamond to engrave glass, but it was in the Northern Alps—in Hall, Tyrol—that the art of diamond engraving was later fostered. In 1573, the Venetian Giacomo Vercellini introduced diamond engraving to England, while in Germany— chiefly around Nuremberg, Saxony and Silesia—it was commonly being used for decoration and for heraldic inscriptions. Dating back to the 16th Century are the Kalligraphengläser, glasses from the Netherlands etched with grand, sweeping initials. There are also the engravings of two sisters, Anna Roemers-Visscher and Maria Tesselschade, together with the work of Anna Maria von Schuermann and Willem Jacobsz von Heemskerk from Leyden—not to mention a number of other amateur examples. Anna Roemers-Visscher in particular left behind many fine pieces: glasses etched with contemporary engravings, with linear cross-hatching and Greek and Latin lettering. In the mid-18th Century Kanonikus A. O. E. von dem Busch, from Hildesheim, was staining his engraved glasses with lamp-black. Also during this century Frans Greenwood was beginning to experiment with glass stippling, a technique whereby variously grouped dots, tapped onto the glass with a diamond nib, can be used to exciting effect. The painters David Wolff and Aert Schouman, who mainly worked from their own designs, were two well-known successors towards the end of the 18th Century and there remain many unsigned works to indicate a number of other students of the art. From the first half of this century we have the stippled glasses of D. H. de Castro, but the exclusive art of glass-engraving was then already being superseded by cutting and polishing and indeed the original form was almost forgotten.

Fortunately, however, this elegant and delicate skill has during the last fifty years enjoyed a revival. The name of Gertrud Bohnert, for example, might be particularly well-known to all those who love glass.

Today, easy-to-use diamond needles have made glass engraving a popular pastime, particularly in Switzerland, with all who are fond of beautiful glassware. It is in this country that diamond engraving can now almost be called a 'people's art'. Remarkable achievements are being attained and true masterpieces created.

Glass the material

Glass is formed when a combination of natural products, chiefly silica and alkalis, are melted, mixed and cooled together.

The basic raw material for glass-making is silica earth, or sand. To this is added a flux (usually soda or potash) to lower the melting-point and lengthen the period during which the glass is viscous and malleable. Substances like limestone, calcium carbonate and lead are then added to strengthen the glass and make it shiny and resistant.

All kinds of glass are the same in that they do not have a crystalline structure; glass is a solidified liquid. There are around 300 different types: the constituents are always the same, only the proportions vary. They can be roughly divided into three groups:

Common glass   — calcium and sodium carbonate (soda-lime)
Bohemian glass — potash and calcium
Crystal glass   — lead

Hard and Soft Glass

Glass varies in strength and theoretically every kind can be engraved, but hard glass is more likely to splinter while being worked on and lines tend to be ragged, blunting the needle more quickly and resulting in a dull, grey-white engraving.

Soft glass, on the other hand, can be engraved clearly and easily; wear on the needle is minimal and the result is much more satisfactory, with silky-smooth, white lines. So it is understandable that the glass-engraver is always on the lookout for 'soft' glass.

As a rule crystal (lead) glass is soft, but you can have a nasty surprise if it has been strengthened to make it tough enough for use in a dishwasher, because this causes it to be hard and brittle. The only glass which is guaranteed to be soft—by the addition of borax—is trade-named Pyrex. But here is a hint to avoid misunderstanding: the terms 'hard' or 'soft' tell you nothing about the suitability of the glass for engraving, only about its melting point in the manufacturing process.

Coloured Glass

Only some types of coloured glass are suitable for engraving, i.e.:

Ruby glass   — red coloured
Amber glass   — yellow coloured
Burnished glass — variegated/lustrous

The following are unsuitable for engraving:
Through-coloured glass, i.e. wine and beer bottles.
Coated glass, i.e. white glass which has been covered with one or more layers of coloured glass.

Ruby glass is coated with an extremely thin film of red colouring, which penetrates the outer layer of the glass and bonds to it. The same is true of amber glass. Both can be identified by the colourless (transparent, white) undersurface.

Ruby glass is formed from crystal, which is coated with copper oxide and baked three times; amber glass undergoes the same process, but with a coating of quicksilver. Both are expensive and very beautiful.

Burnished glass is made by painting the surface with a variety of different colours and then baking the glass in a kiln. It can usually be identified by its metallic sheen and the rainbow-effect of its colouring.

Left: crystal glass.   Centre: ruby glass.   Right: amber glass.

These three different kinds of glass can all be diamond engraved. The etched area is, of course, white and the effect is quite beautiful.

Decorative table bell.

Whisky tumbler.

Confectionery jar.

Tumbler.

Burnished glass pendants. Here too, the engraved areas are white, but because the glass distances the image on the back the effect is enhanced.

There is nothing to be gained from engraving through-coloured glass, for the obvious reason that there will be no tonal variation between image and background. Coated glass is useful for cutting and polishing, but a diamond needle will not pierce the coating, even if it is very thin. Once again, therefore, there would be no tonal difference in the engraving.

Shapes of glass and types of pattern

You should always choose the pattern to suit the type of glass. For example, on a thick, heavy glass you would use a bold design, while fine, delicate glass needs a fine motif.

Initialled glasses. The one in the middle has been engraved correctly. On the others, the design is positioned either too high or too low.

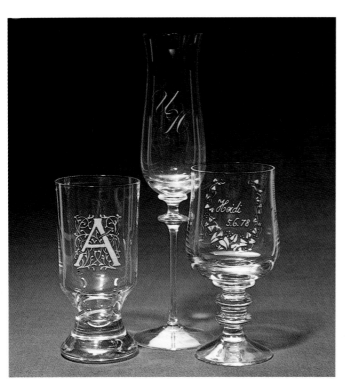

It is important that the design is the right size and positioned correctly to match the shape of the glass. A large glass can accommodate a sizeable motif, but a little one requires something smaller. Always remember that fine engravings are as effective on small glasses as on large, but more heavily-shaded designs will not be so effective on smaller items.

The design too small—too big.

On the large glass the dragonfly looks very effective, but on the small one its fine lines are swallowed up by the reflection.

You should be able to read the whole monogram from one side. If there is not enough room, reduce the size and reposition the design; that way it will look neater and lighter.

The form of the motif should complement the shape of the glass, i.e. square glass, square motif! Glasses with heavy bottoms can 'swallow' the engraving, so with these you should set the design about 2 cms above the thickened base. Always pay attention to the way the glass has been made: those with polished or cut lower halves distort the engraving and can ruin your entire design.

On a round, bowl-shaped glass an ornate, sweeping initial looks more appropriate.
On the right, the engraving has been half-absorbed by the heavy base of the glass.

With jugs and tankards you can really impress your guests. One moment they have a blank glass in front of them, the next they turn it around and find an initial, a date, or even a dedication on the other side—unless, of course, it has been engraved all the way around.

The important part of the motif should be on the visible side.

If you want to repeat a design, engrave it three or four
times around the object.

If you want to engrave more than one design on a glass, there is one important rule to follow: never engrave two different designs on opposite sides of the glass (i.e. a bunch of grapes on one side a monogram on the other) because they will almost certainly clash. In the case of the above-mentioned example, it would be better to incorporate the monogram into the larger grape motif. Only symmetrical designs can really be engraved opposite one another.

Here, the initials have been correctly incorporated into the larger design.

The exception, a symmetrical design repeated on the reverse side of the bowl.

Borders and branches can be engraved all the way round the glass to form a highly decorative effect.

These bowls are very valuable and such intricate engraving requires a great deal of time and patience.

Cut-flowers and bouquets drawn vertically appear stiff and awkward, but engraved obliquely they look alive and natural.

The same rose: on the left natural and elegant, on the right stiff and lifeless because it has been drawn vertically.

When you have a little more experience you can be more discerning in your choice of glass. With higher quality glass, your work becomes more delicate and will naturally be greatly appreciated and worth even more.

Plants and flowers in a natural growing form, on the other hand, must stand upright.

A Place to Work

Your work surface should be soft, like a cushion or mat, and dark-coloured, with a covering of velvet, felt or wool. Try to avoid patterned or shiny material, which reflects light and tires the eyes.

Much of the time you cannot rest your hand on either the table or the glass. This is difficult and makes steadying your work a problem. Try using a book to support your hand or rest the glass in the hollow of a cushion or in a piece of hollowed-out polystyrene.

The Work Surface

The most important pre-requisite is good lighting, ideally daylight or a good table lamp. A bright ceiling light is not adequate. From the very beginning work on a table and not on your knees—it will save you from backache! If you develop a pain in your wrist, this probably means you are pressing too hard.

Magnifying Glass

A reasonable size glass engraving will not harm the eyes, but after a while, of course, close work will tire them. A magnifying glass with an adjustable arm therefore comes in very useful for fine engraving. Steer clear of magnifying glasses with lights attached, because these cause reflections; and avoid those which hang around your neck—they are usually more of a hindrance than a help.

Duster

Never blow away the glass dust. Similarly, do not brush it away with your fingers, because the natural oils of your skin will remain on the glass and darken the lines of the engraving. Always use a soft duster or a paper tissue.

Tension Gauge

The 1-2 cms below the rim of a glass could well be under tension and this area should never be engraved, because it breaks very easily. To identify exactly where the tension begins it is possible to buy a tension gauge.

The tools

The most common diamond drills nowadays are those used by dentists, but there are great differences between the various types, as determined by the way in which the splinters of diamond are embedded in the head of the tool. Badly-made needles are poorly set and the diamond grains very easily come loose.

The needles most suitable for glass engraving are those obtained from reputable established sources. These are precision-made with very fine materials and are recognizable by their characteristic markings. There are a variety of different types, for use with all kinds of glass and for all aspects of engraving. They have good, strong tips and can be held firmly in the claw-grip holder, preventing the diamond from slipping and so giving the needle a longer life: because you do not need to keep changing the tip you can work with it right up until the last diamond-splinter has been used. Because the ball-head, as opposed to the diamond point, needle is the most commonly-used, the finer the head the more obvious the point of application on the glass. This is not to say that it is not possible to produce fine engravings with a large needle, but that requires a great deal of practice and sensitivity.

It is very difficult to say how long a diamond needle will last; it depends upon the type of glass you use, how you work on it and the quality of your tool. But do not be deceived by inferior needles or cheaper options like titanium or wolfram, because they have proved to be extremely unsuccessful, more often than not splitting the surface of the glass.

The Toolkit

The following tools will provide you with all you need for successful glass engraving:

Standard ballpoint needle. In three sizes: small, medium and large.

Carborundum. Not a diamond, but a whetstone; used to smooth and finish ground surfaces.

Tools for Advanced Students

For the advanced student there is a further selection of specialist tools; for example:

Diamond flame. Having a granulated head. With the tip you can produce fine lines, but when used on an angle this tool enables you to work over a wider area with several diamond splinters.

Diamond point. A firm favourite. Because the head is conical you can see and work on your chosen object with particular ease.

Special ballpoint. In three sizes, like the standard ballpoint: small, medium and large. With its ultra-fine head you can produce, particularly on hard or brittle glass, very fine lines; it is easier to produce varying shades. However, it wears out more quickly and tends to become clogged with dust more often, requiring regular cleaning.

Exclusive miniature ballhead. The smallest head of all with very fine diamond-grains.

Velour glass rubber. By using this to slightly roughen the surface of the glass, you can prevent the needle from slipping.

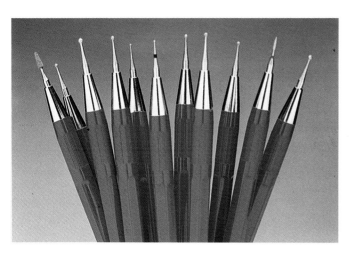

Chinagraph pencil. A white wax crayon, with which you can draw your design directly onto the glass. This white sketch will give you a good idea of how the finished engraving will look and is easily wiped off afterwards.

White copying paper. Used to trace the motif on to the glass. Always use the outside surface of the object, never the interior.

Acrylic tools. These come in two types: flame tips and arrow tips. Only to be used with acrylic. Wear on the head is negligible.

The design has been sketched with a chinagraph pencil to give an impression of the finished engraving. The drawing can now be followed with a needle.

Glass engraving in practice

To be successful at glass engraving you must first appreciate that it is fundamentally different from ordinary drawing. You always etch that which is light: that is to say, the engraved areas are white and the unetched areas dark.

wrong   right

wrong   right

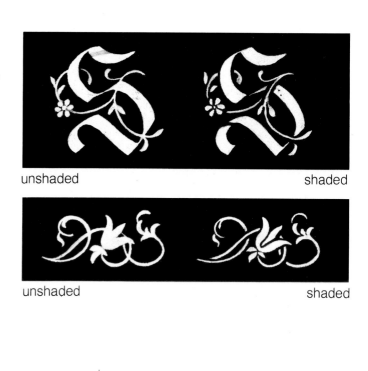

unshaded   shaded

unshaded   shaded

The secret of good engraving lies in what is left un-engraved. The only exceptions are initials and ornamental designs, which naturally cannot be shaded so effectively because much of the motif would then disappear.

wrong

right

There are, to date, many different types of patterns available and new ones are appearing all the time. You can find them in many craft or hobby shops.

If you do want to make your own pattern, do it with a white crayon on black paper. It is not enough merely to draw the outlines; the whole motif must be filled in so that you are sure of what to leave unetched when shading your engraving.

If you decide to use a postcard, fancy wrapping paper, or other material as a pattern, it is best to take a black pen and mark all those areas which are to be left un-engraved.

Different engraving methods

Line Drawing

Line drawing is the oldest glass engraving technique. The surface is 'hatched', which means that you engrave parallel lines running in the same direction throughout the motif. This technique can be applied with or without outlines.

Line drawing is used primarily for stylised motifs, ornamental work and lettering.

Stippling

The stippled effect is achieved by tapping the surface of the glass lightly with the needle. The result is a series.of white dots which can be built, through careful grouping, into a motif. This particular method is extremely time-consuming and stippled glassware can therefore be very expensive.

Space Engraving

This is the technique whereby whole areas of glass are etched white: varying depths of engraving result in varying shades of white.

Examples of glasses engraved only in white.

Lettering, decorations and stylised designs can be engraved entirely in white, but to achieve a realistic effect the white should be shaded.

◁ *Only the figure of Cupid has been stippled, the rest of the design has been engraved in the normal way.*

Perfect engravings with graduated white shading

The Fling Stroke

To complete the list of techniques we come to the fling stroke, ideal for such things as ears of corn, animal fur and whiskers or the covering up of mistakes!

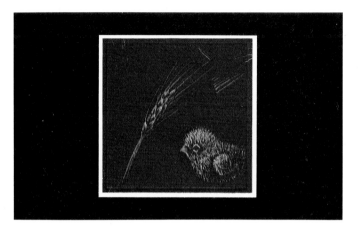

The Total Picture

All the foregoing techniques are combined to create the best possible design.

Perfect engravings with graduated white shading.

Hints, Tips and Tricks

Because glass is a hard substance people not surprisingly think that it requires force and pressure to work on it. But this is not the case. On the contrary, glass should be treated very gently and delicately.

White toning

Instead of colours, in glass-engraving you work with various 'shades' of white, which are produced by removing the surface of the glass by degrees.

To obtain this 'shaded' effect, follow these simple instructions:

1. Hold the needle upright in your hand and gently work it over the glass in a parallel motion: the result is a barely visible shading. It is a little like using a pencil.

2. By going over the lines again in the same direction this almost transparent surface becomes lighter.

Jug, engraved using a combination of techniques.

3. From now on keep repeating the process and slowly but surely the surface will gradually turn white.

4. To obtain a pure white, or to smooth the surface, rub over the engraved area with the carborundum.

To achieve a fine, silky-white finish you must etch the surface of the glass, not only without exerting too much pressure, but also without leaving any gaps—all the empty spaces must be covered. The easiest way to do this is to fill in the engraved area with a series of parallel lines: lay down a basic framework (almost like a barred window) and then slowly cover the entire surface by filling in the ever narrowing spaces between the lines. Always work in the same direction. If you criss-cross lines diagonally or horizontally you will end up with an

unattractive grating-like effect, and this can also damage your needle.

Neat outlines

To ensure neat outlines always work from the contour inwards or along the length of your design.

If you etch across your motif you can easily run over the

outline. Circular or arched designs are dealt with in exactly the same way.

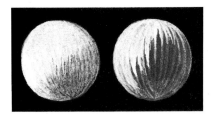 

Engraving flat objects

Dishes, plates, trays and pendants can also be engraved in reverse; but be careful with initials and lettering! These should be traced onto the glass so that they read the right way round when engraved. Pattern sheets may be used in the normal way or by tracing down, dependent on which way the design looks more effective. Remember, however, that with plates made from burnished or ruby glass you cannot engrave in reverse; you can only work on the coloured surface itself.

A particularly interesting effect is gained by engraving the lighter, brighter areas of the motif on both sides of the glass.

On this dish the lighter areas have been engraved on both sides, giving an interesting shadow dimension.

Three-dimensional engraving

An especially attractive and lifelike effect can be produced by etching part of your engraving on the front of an object and part on the back. Again, use a wax crayon to sketch on the front what you want to engrave on the back. This technique can unfortunately only be used on flat objects.

Three-dimensional effect achieved by engraving partly on the front of an object and partly on the back.

▷

Straight lines

To ensure that lines are straight, stick a piece of adhesive tape to the glass and draw along the edge, or use a ruler holding it slightly raised from the surface.

Empty spaces

To avoid accidently engraving eyes, mouths, stamens or other delicate parts of a design, cover up these areas after you have drawn the contour with pieces of sticky paper.

Engraving jars

Before engraving a jar or glassware that has a lid, be sure that your design will not come too close to the rim, because then you will not be able to see the whole motif clearly when you put the lid on.

A useful hint: if you buy a jar or other item and later find that it is slightly chipped, remember that a little stippling will cover up the damage.

Designs which run too close to the lid of the jar tend to be spoilt.

Mistakes

Mistakes cannot be erased, but they can be disguised with decoration. Try out a few ideas with the chinagraph pencil: with a little imagination you can turn a mistake into an interesting part of the design.

Interpreting the pattern

Even though it is recommended that you work with a pattern, you can still give your engraving a personal touch. It is surprising what different results can be obtained using the same design. It all depends on your own personal creative approach.

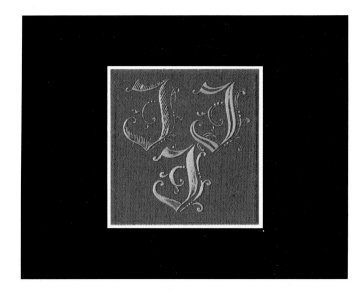

Initials, too, can be engraved in all sorts of interesting ways.

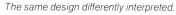

The same design differently interpreted.

Flaws in the glass

Even the most expensive glasses are seldom completely flawless, since they are invariably handmade. As the famous book on glass, *Sevres Crystal*, points out, "Irregularities and minor imperfections are unavoidable and provide irrefutable proof that the glass is handmade" Look carefully at each glass. Usually you can absorb a flaw into your design or cover it up with your engraving. Never leave a flaw close to a motif, because the imperfection will then be more obviously accentuated.

Coloured engravings

Glass engravings can be 'painted' by using transparent tints or coloured pastes.

With normal transparent glass one of the most interesting effects is achieved by using black paste, which gives the glass a similar appearance to an etching. White paste, too, can be used to accentuate your engraving and is particularly useful when decorating a pendant to highlight the motif against your clothes.

Unfortunately, gold or silver paste is not quite as suitable for transparent glass because from the back it does not look so interesting, but with ruby and through-coloured glass (although the latter is not strictly-speaking suitable for engraving) it can be used to great effect.

Transparent colouring and engraving.

Transparent tinting and engraving.

The engraving on this pendant is highlighted by the white paste.

Engraving etched with coloured paste.

Black burnished glass pendant, with partially-coloured engraving.

Machine engraving

For initials and decorative work it is possible to use a machine, but most machines are expensive and in any case it is much more satisfying to work by hand.

So we begin

Working with a pattern

Choose a glass and a suitable pattern.

inner surface and secure it with scotch tape; it is also a good idea to pack the glass with a tissue or some paper to hold the pattern in place.

Take the fine needle and, without using too much pressure, draw the outlines of the pattern. You will feel the diamond scratching the glass. Work systematically and be sure not to go over the same line twice. When you have finished remove the packing and pattern.

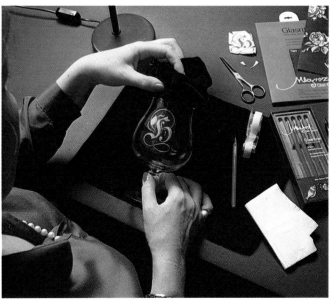

Cut out your chosen motif and make one or two small incisions in the sides so that it will lie more snugly against the curve of the glass. Then position the pattern on the

Slowly the design will take shape. From time to time you will need to clean the needle, because it tends to get clogged with the ink from your tracing: to do this, hold the tip between finger and thumb and gently revolve the point. When you have finished etching the outline, wipe clean the surface with a soft cloth.

Now the preparations are over and you can start on the engraving proper. Remember all the hints and tips in the last chapter and try interpreting or adapting the pattern to achieve the results you want.

From now on you have a choice of tools, ranging from the basic needles to the more specialised ones we mentioned earlier.

Tracing

You cannot always stick a pattern to the inside of the glass. With narrow-necked bottles, bulbs or pendants you have to trace the motif, and for this you will need some white copying paper. Do not try to use common tracing paper—it is too stiff and thick.

Cut the copying paper to size and, as before, make some small incisions in the sides. Place the shiny side against the glass and lay the pattern on top securing both with scotch tape; you can now use a sharpened hard pencil to trace the design onto the glass. When you have finished, remove both pattern and copying paper.

Using the fine needle, engrave over the traced design, remembering if you are right-handed to begin on the right side of the motif, so that you do not rub off the pattern.

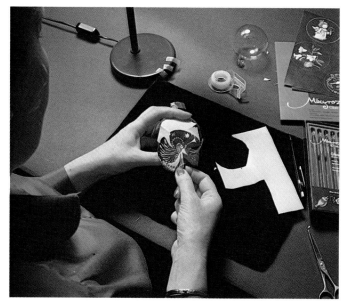

The following general rules apply:
Contour or fine needle for outlines.
Fine needle for delicate lines.
Medium or large needle, depending upon the size of the surface to be engraved, for the more solid parts of the motif.

As we have already stated, you can work more economically with the larger needles, but more precisely with the finer ones. For particularly fine engravings, however, you really need the special ballpoint (equipped with ultra-fine splinters of diamond and identifiable by special markings) which also comes in three sizes, or the flame-headed needle we mentioned earlier.

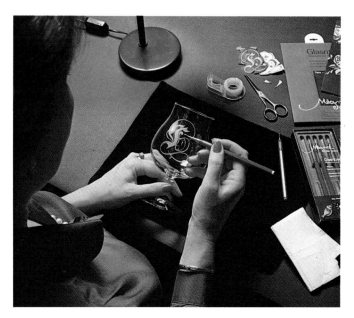

Engraving acrylic

Acrylic or 'flexiglass' is an art material and can be engraved without difficulty. Because it is soft it is easy to work on and is therefore ideal for children, but it also has fascinating possibilities for adults.

Acrylic is easy to engrave, but it is also easily scratched, so be careful when cleaning away the dust: never rub it off, but dab it away with cotton wool.

You can work on acrylic with the same pattern that you use on ordinary glass, since the problems of light and shading are the same. Draw your motif on the object with the recommended special needle, following the pattern just as you do when you are engraving glass, or using copying paper if necessary. If you want to prime the surface first, an ordinary pencil rubber is ideal.

Acrylic is engraved in much the same way as ordinary glass: the acrylic flame-headed needle is best for contours and sharp lines, while the arrowhead needle is perfect for dots and fling strokes.

You can colour your engraving very easily by gently rubbing over the motif with a pencil or crayon. If you then carefully clean the surface with cotton wool, the colouring will be left in the etched areas of your design. To effectively reproduce hair, fur or down, prepare the surface first with a glass-fibre brush or some steel wool.

You can then draw in individual hairs with the needle. By engraving an acrylic disc, which you can mould yourself, you can make a charming little cameo. If you then cover it with a piece of protective glass, frame it in a

band of lead or pewter (commercially available for this purpose) and make a small hole at the top with a hot needle, you will have a beautiful pendant.

There are as yet comparatively few fancy acrylic objects on the market, but you can buy cheese- and butter-dishes, tongs, salt-cellars, salad spoons, paperweights, etc., all of which can be exquisitely decorated with a little thought and imagination.

Suggestions

This book has attempted to show you how to work with glass and produce attractive engravings. We have looked at many technically and aesthetically interesting patterns and engravings, but you have also learned how to create your own special design.

Personalised Venetian decanter.

Coat-of-arms on a ruby decanter.

A jug with ornamental initials.

Liqueur decanter decorated with a bunch of cherries.

Ruby wedding goblet decorated with an old Swiss wedding-scene.

Hanging Easter egg and Christmas tree balls.

Glass-engraving, if approached with care, offers a particularly special way of personalising your gifts, whether it be with family coats-of-arms, names, initials or an appropriate design. You can decorate glasses, decanters, vases, plates and trays with motifs for weddings, christenings, jubilees, birthdays and festivals like Christmas and Easter.

Decorate your own table with personalised glasses, trays, dishes and tableware; or engrave glass Easter eggs or Christmas tree balls with motifs of your choice.

Give a friend or relative a glass with his or her name on it as a birthday present. Animal-lovers will be delighted to receive an engraving of their favourite pet. You can even personalise your guests' napkin-rings on special occasions so that they can take them away as souvenirs. We could go on and on with the list of possibilities. Only your imagination sets the limits on what you can do. And not only will your new hobby give you many hours of pleasure but will also earn you the admiration of your friends.

Engraved perfume bottles.

A decorated glass jewel-case.

Personalised glasses for children.